J BIOGRAPHY ARISTOTLE
Anderson, Margaret J.
Aristotle

Not AR

GREAT MINDS OF SCIENCE

Aristotle
Philosopher and Scientist

JUL   2006

Margaret J. Anderson and
Karen F. Stephenson

Enslow Publishers, Inc.
40 Industrial Road   PO Box 38
Box 398   Aldershot
Berkeley Heights, NJ 07922 Hants GU12 6BP
USA   UK
http://www.enslow.com

Library of Congress Cataloging-in-Publication Data

Anderson, Margaret J.
    Aristotle : philosopher and scientist / Margaret J. Anderson and Karen
F. Stephenson.
      v. cm. — (Great minds of science)
    Contents: Living in interesting times — Aristotle's childhood — Athens,
the City of Wonder — The Academy — A new direction — The Father of
Zoology — Alexander — The Lyceum — "A Desire for Knowledge"— The
end of the road — His writings live on — Aristotle's influence.
   ISBN 0-7660-2096-7
    1. Aristotle—Juvenile literature. 2. Scientists—Greece—Biography—
Juvenile literature. 3. Philosophers—Greece—Biography—Juvenile litera-
ture. [1. Aristotle. 2. Scientists. 3. Philosophers.] I. Stephenson, Karen F.
II. Title. III. Series.
Q143.A65A53 2004
185—dc21

                                    2003002270

Printed in the United States of America

10 9 8 7 6 5 4 3

To Our Readers:
We have done our best to make sure all Internet Addresses in this book were
active and appropriate when we went to press. However, the author and the
publisher have no control over and assume no liability for the material
available on those Internet sites or on other Web sites they may link to. Any
comments or suggestions can be sent by e-mail to comments@enslow.com or
to the address on the back cover.

Illustration Credits: ArtToday.com, pp. 43, 47, 49, 52, 79, 83, 93, 98;
Corel Corporation, pp. 22, 24, 26, 27; David Torsiello/Enslow
Publishers, Inc., pp. 32, 86; Dover Pictorial Archives, p. 45; Enslow
Publishers, Inc., pp. 9, 17, 35, 56, 64, 76; Library of Congress, pp. 11,
68, 90.

Cover Illustration: Corel Corporation (background); David
Torsiello/Enslow Publishers, Inc. (inset).

Contents

Living in Interesting Times

MOST PEOPLE TODAY DO NOT THINK OF philosophy as a very exciting subject. Advances in genetics, physics, and medicine make headlines. New ideas in philosophy seldom do. Part of the reason for this may be due to the uncertain nature of philosophy. The field of philosophy deals with questions about the meaning of life and the natures of justice and truth. Because there are no definite answers to these questions, people seldom discuss philosophy over their coffee breaks or lunch.

That is not the way people felt in ancient Greece, however. Back then, people had many hot debates and noisy arguments over philosophy. Being a philosopher could put a person in jeopardy. Philosophers were often run out of town. Some were even put to death for what they believed.

Athens was the center of ancient Greek philosophy. No other place in the ancient world valued knowledge and learning more than Athens. In fact, the city was named for Athena, the Greek goddess of wisdom. Athens was the home of some of the greatest artists and philosophers in the history of the Western world. Among them were the philosophers Socrates, Plato, and Aristotle, who lived there in the fifth and fourth centuries B.C. The city's democratic form of government—which goes all the way back to 508 B.C.—has been a model for lawmakers ever since. As a result, many people consider Athens to be the birthplace of Western civilization.

In 431 B.C., Athens entered into a long war with the city-state of Sparta. This conflict, known as the Peloponnesian War, lasted almost thirty years and ended with Athens being conquered.

In 404 B.C., the city's democratic form of government was overthrown. A group of men, known as the Thirty Tyrants, became the rulers. Although democracy was restored about a year later, these were troubled times.

During this period, Socrates was a teacher in Athens. From the beginning, Socrates was different from other teachers. Other philosophers mostly concerned themselves with the origins of the universe, but Socrates was more concerned with peoples' character. He encouraged the young men of Athens to question the current ideas of justice. This led to the charge that he was corrupting the young. He also drew attention to himself by refusing to recognize the traditional Greek gods and goddesses. He talked about having his own "guardian spirit."[1] This sounded to his accusers as if he were introducing a new god, which was considered a crime.

Socrates was brought to trial before an assembly of 500 Athenians. His fellow citizens found him guilty of corrupting the young men of Athens. As punishment, the assembly ordered that Socrates be put to death by drinking a brew of hemlock—a poisonous herb.

It happened that a fleet of sacred ships had set sail the day before Socrates was sentenced. The people of Athens were afraid that an execution at that particular time might offend the gods, so Socrates was kept in prison until the ships returned.[2] During the month he was a prisoner, his friends and family were allowed to visit him. One of his friends came up with a plan to help him to escape, but Socrates refused to go along with it. He insisted that the first duty of a citizen is to obey the laws of his city, even when the laws are unjust. He said that one injustice could not be put right with another injustice.[3] When the day of his execution finally arrived, the aged philosopher took the cup of poison and drained it calmly. His friends and family looked on and wept.

Socrates is one of the greatest philosophers the world has known. Plato, his student, became equally famous. Plato greatly admired—almost worshipped—Socrates. When he became a teacher at the Academy, Plato passed on the

This painting depicts Socrates as he is about to take his cup of poison. Surrounding friends and family look away, as they cannot bear to watch him drink it.

great philosopher's wisdom to all his own students. He also passed it on to later generations through his writing. Like Socrates, Plato also had one particularly brilliant student. This student was Aristotle. Aristotle went on to become perhaps the most famous and influential philosopher of all time.

Although he lived nearly twenty-four hundred years ago, Aristotle is still respected as a scientist, writer, and teacher. Over the course of his life, he studied and wrote about every field of knowledge then imaginable. He studied physics, zoology, botany, and chemistry before any of these fields of science even had names. He believed that "the wise man must not only be able to draw deductions from first principles, but must also have a true knowledge of the first principles themselves. Hence wisdom is . . . a combination of intelligence and scientific understanding."[4]

In Aristotle's time, science was considered a branch of philosophy. Even as late as the seventeenth century, when Isaac Newton discovered the law of gravity, physics was still called "natural philosophy." The word *philosophy* comes from two Greek words: *philo*, meaning "love," and *sophia*, meaning "knowledge." So *philosophy* actually means "love of knowledge."

Aristotle's life was built on the search for knowledge. In addition to his work in science, he contributed a great deal to our ideas about art, literature, ethics (moral values), and theology (the study of God and religious faith). Aristotle's

The ancient philosopher and scientist Aristotle.

influence is so deep, in fact, that many of his ideas have been absorbed into the very language of science and philosophy. Without question, this marks Aristotle as one of the most significant figures in all of history.

With so many famous people around, the fourth century B.C. was an interesting time to be alive. Another great figure of history who lived during that period was Alexander of Macedonia—better known as Alexander the Great. On the surface, Aristotle and Alexander would seem to be very different men. Aristotle was a teacher and philosopher. Alexander was one of the most famous conquerors in history. Despite this, the two men played key roles in one another's lives.

In 343 B.C., King Philip of Macedonia—a country to the north of Greece—asked Aristotle to teach his thirteen-year-old son, Alexander. By this time, Aristotle had spent a lot of time studying natural history and had written many books. He had much to offer his lively, intelligent pupil. In addition to teaching him about plants and animals, Aristotle gave the young prince a love of the works of the Greek poet, Homer.

When Alexander was sixteen, he moved on to a new phase of his education. He joined his father's army and Aristotle was no longer needed. Four years later, King Philip died. Twenty-year-old Alexander took over as King of Macedonia. One of Alexander's first acts as king was to march against the neighboring country of Persia. He then went on to more ambitious conquests. Eventually, he led his conquering army all the way to India.

While on his travels, Alexander took the time to send Aristotle examples of any unusual plants and animals that he came across. By then, Aristotle was head of his own school in Athens. He set up a museum in his school to display the specimens that Alexander sent to him.[5]

When Alexander died at the age of thirty-three, the countries and cities he had conquered turned against Macedonia. One of the cities Alexander had controlled was Athens. After Alexander's death, the citizens of Athens showed their anger by driving out anyone who had any connection with the famous conqueror. This, of course, included Aristotle.

Fearing that he would share the fate of Socrates if he stayed in Athens, Aristotle fled to an island in the Aegean Sea. He did not want Athens to go down in history as the city where two great philosophers had been sentenced to death. In his words, he said he left Athens to keep the city from "sinning twice against philosophy."[6]

Aristotle's Childhood

ARISTOTLE WAS BORN IN 384 B.C. IN Stagira, a small town in northern Greece. He had one brother and one sister. His father, Nicomachus, was a successful doctor. His mother, Phaestis, came from the island of Euboea to the south. Aristotle's mother was a person of some wealth. The house she owned in Euboea remained in the family after she married Nicomachus.[1] It was there that Aristotle fled upon the death of Alexander the Great.

Because Aristotle lived so long ago, it is impossible to know many details of his personal life. One of his biographers was a Greek historian named Diogenes Laertius. His book provides the only description that we have of Aristotle. It is not very flattering. Diogenes tells us that the philosopher spoke with a lisp. He claims that "his calves were slender (so they say), his eyes small, and he was conspicuous by his attire, his rings, and the cut of his hair."[2]

Diogenes lived in the third century A.D.—about 500 years after Aristotle died—so this description may not be accurate. We can put more trust in what we can learn from Aristotle's own writing or in facts that are recorded by several writers. We can also learn something about Aristotle by looking at what life was like in Greece in those days for a person of his education.[3]

Boys usually went to privately run community schools when they were about six years old. There they were taught reading, writing, and arithmetic. They practiced writing by scratching letters with a pointed stick on a wax-coated wooden block. Mistakes could just be scraped off. When the wax wore down, a new coat was

A map of Greece and the surrounding territories in the time of Aristotle.

applied. Arithmetic was taught using pebbles and an abacus (a counting board).

When boys grew older, music and poetry were added to the curriculum. They learned to play the lyre (a small type of harp) and the flute. Homer's long poems, the *Iliad* and the *Odyssey*, were their texts. Students learned lengthy passages by heart. At around the age of fourteen, they took up sports and dancing. The most popular sport was wrestling. By this time boys were also studying geometry, literature, and rhetoric. Rhetoric is the art of giving speeches. The ability to sway people with words was the mark of an educated person in ancient Greece.

Girls did not usually have the opportunity to learn to read and write. They learned at home from their mothers, who taught them to spin, to weave, and to cook. They tended to marry young, around the age of fourteen or fifteen. The typical role of a woman was to make clothes, prepare meals, and raise children. A woman spent most of her time at home. The man of the house shopped at the marketplace and often entertained his male friends at dinner parties in the evening.

Aristotle may have learned to read and write along with other children at the local school, but it is likely that his father, the doctor, also taught him at home. The practice of medicine was handed down within families from father to son. Only the supposed descendants of Asclepias, the god of healing, could take up medicine.

The education of a future doctor began early. Watching his father examine his patients may have sparked Aristotle's interest in human anatomy. Nicomachus probably took his son along when he went out in search of healing plants. The young boy would probably have been an eager student, judging from his later interest in biology. Perhaps his later love of plants and animals also grew out of this early training.

Nicomachus must have been a good and respected doctor. While Aristotle was still a child, his father was invited to become the personal doctor to King Amyntas II of Macedonia. We do not know if the whole family moved to the royal court, but it seems likely that they did. The king's youngest son, Philip, was the same age as Aristotle. Thirty years later, Philip hired Aristotle to tutor his son Alexander. This would seem to support the idea that Philip and Aristotle had known one another as boys.[4]

King Amyntas spent much of his time fighting rebellious princes. The royal physician did not have an easy life. As court doctor, Nicomachus was expected to travel to the battlefield with the army. He died when Aristotle was about ten years old. His wife Phaestis seems to have died around this same time. Aristotle was left an orphan.

The death of his father put an end to Aristotle's prospects for a career in medicine. A relative, Proxenus of Atarneus, became his guardian. Aristotle's life took off in a new direction. He studied rhetoric and poetry. Not much is known about Aristotle's early teenage years, but he remained on good terms with Proxenus throughout his life. In his will, he left instructions for the making of an image of Proxenus.[5]

The death of King Amyntas was followed by a period of civil war and unrest in Macedonia. The court remained in a state of upheaval for several years.[6] Perhaps that was why, when Aristotle was seventeen, Proxenus sent him to Athens to continue his education. It turned out to be a wise choice. At the Academy, young Aristotle was exposed to the wisdom of the great philosopher, Plato.

Athens, the City of Wonder

THE BEGINNING OF GREEK CIVILIZATION goes back to the Minoans. They lived over 4,000 years ago on islands south of the Greek mainland. They were a creative and cultured people. So were the Myceneans, who followed them. Then, around 1100 B.C., the Dorians swept down from the north, destroying the southern towns and bringing in a dark age that lasted for about 300 years.

By 500 B.C., city-states had sprung up all over Greece. A city-state consisted of a city surrounded by small villages and farmland. The city was usually built around a high hill or *acropolis*.

(*Acropolis* means "a high place in the city.") City-states were important political units. They were almost like small, separate nations. Each one had its own form of government. They traded back and forth. They established their own colonies along the shores of the Mediterranean and Aegean Seas. They often fought with one another, although they became allies when countries outside Greece threatened them.

Athens was one of the most beautiful cities in the ancient world. To the seventeen-year-old youth from the north, it must have been a source of wonder. A hundred years earlier, artists,

A modern-day view of the Greek city of Athens.

sculptors, craftsmen, and laborers had created some of the world's most magnificent buildings. No expense had been spared. Marble, bronze, ivory, gold, and rare woods were used as building materials. A stone staircase wound up the side of the Acropolis to a huge pillared entryway. Three temples stood on the summit. The greatest of these was the Parthenon, with seventeen columns along the sides and eight columns in front. Inside was a magnificent statue of Athena, the goddess of wisdom. It stood forty feet high and was made of ivory and gold.[1] The statue is gone now, but the ruins of the temple still stand.

The huge Theater of Dionysus was at the bottom of the hill. Spectators sat in a semicircle on stone benches built into the hillside.[2] Because of the hot, dry climate, there was no need for a roof. Women as well as men formed the audience, but only men could be actors.

The main marketplace, or *agora*, was an open space where farmers and craftsmen set up stalls to sell their wares. The *agora* was surrounded by column-lined walkways, where men met with one

The stone ruins of the Parthenon in Athens.

another to discuss the business of the day or to listen to wandering teachers and orators. The Academy, where Aristotle became a student, was more modest than the city's public buildings. Classes were mostly held outdoors, with the students gathering around their teacher in a rather informal setting.

Athens had a democratic form of government. The word democracy comes from the Greek words *demos* for "people" and *kratia* for "rule." The democratic system was so successful that many other city-states adopted it. Later in his life, Aristotle wrote a lengthy volume on politics.[3] Many of his views were formed during his student years at the Academy.

As a non-citizen of Athens, Aristotle was classified as a *metic*—a foreigner who did not have the right to vote. Two other large groups who could not vote were women and slaves. Slaves accounted for about one third of the population in Athens. They did most of the work. They were, on the whole, well treated. Some were trusted members of a family. They were sometimes given small wages and could eventually buy their freedom. People were either born into slavery or became slaves after being captured during a war.

The ancient Greeks were a proud race. They looked down on outsiders and described foreigners as barbarians. In Book 1 of *Politics*, Aristotle wrote that "war is, in some sense, a part of the art of acquisition (possessing)."[4] He pointed out that it is necessary to hunt wild beasts and went on to say that one also had to use war "against those of mankind who, being

The ruins of an ancient Greek theater.

intended by nature for slavery, are unwilling to submit to it. On this occasion, such a war is by nature just."[5]

Those who were fortunate enough not to be either slaves or women had the leisure to study and take part in sports and games. Men devoted a lot of their time to politics. Athens had a two-part government, the Council and the Assembly. The Council consisted of 500 members who were chosen by lot. It made the laws. The Assembly discussed and voted on the laws. Every citizen had the right to speak and vote at the Assembly, which met every ten days. At least 6,000 citizens had to be present for the meeting to take place.[6] If too few people showed up, the police were sent out to round up more citizens.

The form of democracy practiced in Athens made it possible for the great minds of the time to blossom. When Aristotle came to Athens to study, he got more than just the chance to go to school. He was given the opportunity to learn and grow in the presence of other great minds.

Market stalls as they appear on the streets of present-day Athens.

4

The Academy

WHEN ARISTOTLE ARRIVED IN ATHENS IN 367 B.C., the Academy was only twenty years old, but it was already a famous center of learning. Its founder, the philosopher Plato, was still the director. His philosophy was closely tied to the teachings of Socrates. Forty years earlier, when Plato was twenty, he had met the great philosopher and immediately became his devoted student. Socrates had led a very simple life. He wore a ragged cloak and went barefoot. When he saw all the wares that were for sale in the marketplace, he remarked, "How many things I can do without!"[1] Although he had a gentle nature, he was always ready for an argument. His aim was "not to alter his opinion but to get at the truth."[2]

After Socrates' death, Plato left Athens and spent twelve adventure-filled years traveling in Greece, Egypt, Italy, and Sicily. According to one story, he was captured by pirates on his way home from Sicily. He was then sold as a slave and held at ransom.[3] When he finally got safely back to Athens, he was ready to settle down. He had decided to be a teacher.

In ancient Greece, teachers led a wandering life. They held classes in the streets and the marketplace. If they could not gather enough students, they moved on to another city. Plato wanted to try a different approach. He bought a plot of land where he could set up a permanent school. The land had belonged to the hero Academos, so the school became known as the Academy. Classes were mostly held outdoors. The site included a grove of olive trees that provided shade from the hot sun. There were also probably a few buildings that were used for sleeping and dining.

Plato based his philosophy on the idea that everything is present in two forms: the actual form that we can touch and an ideal form. He gave the example of a carpenter who makes tables. The carpenter has the image of a perfect table in his mind. But the tables that he makes never completely measure up to the table he is picturing in his mind, because no piece of wood is perfect. There are always knots or flaws. No two tables are exactly the same down to the last detail. Tables, therefore, exist in two forms: the ideal table and the tables that carpenters actually make.[4]

Plato said that this is true of everything. There are two realities: the idea of a horse and the horses that people ride; the idea of a dog and all the different kinds of dogs people have as pets. Plato believed that the universe had been put together by a divine craftsman. The craftsman looked to the perfect forms and created all the different objects in the universe as copies or images of them.

Students at the Academy focused on just two areas—politics and philosophy. But philosophy was a wide umbrella. It covered subjects such as physics and astronomy. Plato's desire was to give his students a love of knowledge and wisdom. Scholars came from near and far, attracted by Plato himself, as much as by his goals. Because scholars shared their mastery of mathematics, medicine, and astronomy, the Academy was an exciting environment for an eager student. Aristotle certainly fit that description. During his years at the Academy, he earned the nickname Anagnostes, which means "the reader" or "the mind."[5]

With his brilliant mind, Aristotle no doubt shared in the teaching at the Academy, at first as a student, and later as what we might today call a postgraduate student. However, students did not actually graduate from Plato's school. There were no examinations. Young men attended classes to seek wisdom, not to get a degree or to prepare themselves for a career.

At some point, Aristotle rejected Plato's views and developed his own philosophy. Plato is reported to have said, "Aristotle spurns me as colts kick out at the mother who bore them."[6]

A detail from Raphael's School of Athens. *On the left, Plato points upward, symbolizing his view that ideas and eternal forms are the ultimate reality. On the right, Aristotle gestures toward the ground, symbolizing his belief in the natural sciences.*

But the rift between them was probably not serious. In his early writing, Aristotle reflects the views of the Academy, and in his later works, he writes fondly of Plato.

Aristotle preferred to deal only with the visible world. He thought that making two worlds (the ideal world and the visible world) out of one just added to the number of things that needed to be explained. Aristotle did not agree with the idea of a divine craftsman creating the universe out of unformed materials.

Aristotle argued that there are two states: the state of "potential being" and the state of "actual being."[7] He gave the example of an acorn growing into an oak tree, in which the acorn changes from one kind of being to another kind of being. If the timber of the oak is made into a boat, the oak tree changes into yet another form of being.

Aristotle observed that we live in an orderly world. Things in the natural world behave as we expect them to behave. When we plant an acorn, we can expect it to grow into an oak tree and not an apple tree. When a rock is dropped, it always falls down and not up. Rivers flow to the sea and not to the mountaintops.

Aristotle presented a theory to provide an answer to basic questions, such as: Why do rocks fall? Why does water run downhill? Why does smoke go upwards? He proposed that all matter is a mixture of four basic elements: earth, water, fire, and air. Each of these elements is a combination of hot or cold and wet or dry. Earth is cold and dry; water is cold and wet; air is hot and wet; fire is hot and dry. In addition, earth and water are heavy, with earth being heavier than water. Fire and air are light, with fire being lighter than air. If these elements existed in a pure state, earth would be at the center of the universe with a layer of water around it. Beyond that would be air, and finally fire.

Because all substances are a mixture of elements, they do not separate out. Instead they are drawn to their natural place. Rock is the material of earth, therefore it always falls down, back to the earth. Flames shoot up because they are drawn to fire on the outermost level of the

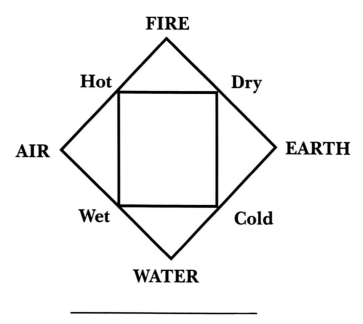

Aristotle's scheme of matter.

universe.[8] This reasoning may sound strange to us today, but Aristotle was basing his conclusions on his own experience and what was known twenty-four hundred years ago.

Aristotle argued that on Earth everything keeps changing. The seasons change. Plants and animals die and decay. On the other hand, the heavens stay the same, generation after generation. The sun, the planets, and the stars follow regular circular paths across the sky. He thought that the unchanging heavens must be composed of a purer element than the earth. He called it "ether." He pictured the universe as a series of clear spheres, or hollow balls, with Earth at its center. The sun and planets were each attached to their own sphere. The outermost sphere held the stars in place.

Aristotle was so respected for his arguments and his wisdom that centuries passed before many of his ideas were challenged. It would be the sixteenth century A.D. before a mathematician and astronomer named Copernicus put forward the idea that Earth circles around the sun and is not the center of the universe.

5

A New Direction

WHEN PLATO DIED, HIS NEPHEW TOOK over as director of the Academy. Aristotle was thirty-seven years old and was a highly respected scholar. It is possible that he felt that he should have been offered the job. This could explain why he abruptly left Athens in 347 B.C.

There may, however, have been another reason. By the middle of the fourth century, Macedonia was becoming a threat to all of Greece. Philip, the youngest son of King Amyntas, was now king. The Macedonians were fierce warriors. Philip was a talented general. Under his leadership, his soldiers became great conquerors. While the Greek city-states were fighting among themselves, the Macedonians overran areas to the north of Greece. Aristotle's birthplace, Stagira, resisted for a time, but was finally conquered.

The citizens of Athens were worried. Feelings against Macedonia ran high. It is quite possible that Aristotle did not see these events in the same light. After all, his father had been a doctor in the Macedonian court. His views, and the fact that he was not a citizen, could have made him unpopular in Athens.[1]

Aristotle set off across the Aegean Sea to Asia Minor. When he arrived at the harbor city of Assos, he was warmly greeted by the ruler, Hermias, whose court in Assos was a center of Greek culture. The two men already knew one another because Hermias had visited the Academy in Athens.

Hermias had risen to great heights from humble beginnings. According to one story, he started out as a slave.[2] Another story has it that he had been a money changer, who became wealthy and powerful.[3] Twenty years earlier, he had seized the throne and had become a tyrant king. In ancient Greece, the word *tyrant* was used for any ruler who had complete power. A tyrant was not always wicked, but a king who can make his own laws often becomes what we now call a "tyrant"—a ruler who abuses his power and wields it unfairly.

Aristotle soon settled down in Assos. He married Hermias's niece, Pythias, and became head of a school similar to the Academy. Aristotle was around thirty-seven when he married. He later wrote that the proper age for a man to marry was thirty-seven, and for a woman, eighteen.[4] So it is likely that Pythias was eighteen when she married Aristotle. They had one daughter, who was also named Pythias. Pythias (the mother) died only ten years after marrying Aristotle. It seems that they were happy together. In his will, Aristotle asked that wherever he was buried, "there the bones of Pythias shall be laid."[5] Aristotle's second wife, Herpyllis, was from Stagira. They had a son, whom they named Nicomachus, after Aristotle's father.

Hermias had remained in power by staying in favor with his mighty neighbor, Persia. But while Aristotle was teaching in Assos, Hermias became friendly with Philip of Macedonia. The Persians did not like the idea of Hermias and Philip being allies. They were afraid that Philip might use Assos as a base for launching an attack on their country. Because of this, they began to plot against Hermias.

The King of Persia invited Hermias to meet with him. Hermias accepted, but the invitation turned out to be a trick to get him to leave the safety of his own court. He was immediately taken prisoner and tortured. Although he would not admit to having done any wrong against the Persians, they crucified him. Aristotle composed a poem praising the dead Hermias. This would later be held against him.

Meanwhile, Aristotle and Pythias, along with several teachers from the school in Assos, moved to the nearby island of Lesbos. The island was the home of a young scholar named Theophrastus, who became Aristotle's close friend. He was fifteen years younger than

Aristotle, but they had overlapping interests. Theophrastus was fascinated by botany (the study of plants). Aristotle was curious about the many different creatures that lived in the coastal waters. With the help of his fellow teachers, students, and even the local fishermen, Aristotle began a detailed study of marine animals. Many of the descriptions in his *History of Animals* are from records that were made around Lesbos and Assos.

Most ancient philosophers gave a lot of thought to the stars. They tended to look down on animals as a subject of study. Even Aristotle felt he had to apologize for his interest in the animal kingdom. But he went on to defend himself by pointing out that animals are much easier to study than stars. Much can be learned from their amazing variety of forms. He wrote, "We therefore must not recoil with childish aversion from the examination of the humbler animals. Every realm of nature is marvelous. . . . If any person thinks the examination of the rest of the animal kingdom an unworthy task, he must hold in like scorn the study of man."[6]

Doctors and other scholars had taken an interest in human anatomy and physiology (the workings of the body) since the time of Hippocrates—a famous Greek doctor born in the fifth century B.C. It is not surprising that Aristotle, the son of a doctor, would also be attracted to those subjects. But his studies were hindered by the fact that there was a religious ban on dissecting the human body. He did dissect animals, however, so he was able to gain some understanding of anatomy. Sometimes he came up with completely wrong answers. For example, he thought that the heart was the center of intelligence and that the brain's main job was to cool the heart. He was not aware of the difference between veins and arteries.

The lack of scientific equipment led Aristotle into other mistakes. There are limits to what can be seen with the naked eye, and Aristotle lived long before the invention of the microscope. He mistakenly thought that some kinds of insects do not have parents. He had seen full-grown adults emerge from rotting plants, from dung, and from the bodies of other animals. We now know

Without the benefit of a microscope, Aristotle arrived at some false conclusions. For example, he mistakenly believed that some moths (like the one above) were born out of wool or woolen clothing.

that such insects actually came from eggs that were too small to see. Aristotle also thought that clothes moths came from wool or from clothes made of wool. He added that the little animals "come in greater numbers if the woolen substances are dusty."[7]

However, it is not by his mistakes that we should judge Aristotle. He is important because he recognized a sense of order and purpose in the animal kingdom. He was the first scientist to attempt to divide animals into groups and classify them.

The Father of Zoology

THE FIRST STEP IN DESCRIBING AN animal's habits or behavior is to know its correct name. Otherwise, the study is of no value to other biologists. That is why Aristotle deserves the title, "Father of Zoology." Zoology is the study and classification of animals. Aristotle named and described over 500 species (kinds) of animals. By doing this, he turned the study of natural history into a science.

Many of Aristotle's descriptions came from his own tireless observations. He also interviewed fishermen and travelers. But he did not believe everything he heard. Ctesias wrote that he had seen a strange animal in India called a *mantichoras* (or *manticore*). It had three rows of teeth, the body of a lion, the face of a human, and a tail that shot poison spikes. When describing the animal, Aristotle added the phrase, "if we are to believe Ctesias."[1]

Aristotle separated animals into "bloodless" and "blooded." His bloodless animals are what we now call invertebrates (animals without backbones). He then divided the bloodless animals into four main groups. The first group

Aristotle rightly doubted the existence of the mythical manticore, pictured above.

was the molluscs, which included animals like the squid and the octopus that are soft on the outside. Next came crabs and crayfish, which have a hard outside that can be crushed. The third group included the snail and the oyster with a hard outside that must be shattered. He called his fourth group insects. This group included spiders and centipedes—creatures that we now distinguish from insects.

Aristotle's blooded animals are what we now call vertebrates (animals with backbones). He divided them into man, birds, four-footed animals that gave birth to live babies (such as dogs and sheep), four-footed animals that laid eggs (lizards and snakes), fish that gave birth to live young (such as dolphins and whales), and fish that laid eggs. Snakes obviously do not fit into the four-footed category, but Aristotle put them there because they are like lizards in so many other ways. He understood the importance of natural groups that depended on several characteristics.

Aristotle realized that separating the animals that live in water from those that live on land would separate some animals that have many features in common. For example, he understood that whales, dolphins, and porpoises were different from fish. He put them in a group that he described as "animals with blowholes." These animals do not lay eggs, but give birth to live babies. They produce milk to feed their young. He was, however, confused about how dolphins breathe. Did they "breathe" water or air? He believed that the dolphin "performs both these processes: he takes in water and

Aristotle correctly understood that certain marine animals such as the dolphin, above, were different from ordinary fish.

discharges it by his blow-hole, and he also inhales air into his lungs."[2] He knew that breathing air was important for the dolphin. He had observed that they could survive for a long time out of the water, but that they drowned when they were trapped underwater in fishermen's nets.

Aristotle's descriptions of animals were often lively and make for interesting reading. Here is what he has to say about the octopus:

> *The octopus is a stupid creature, for it will approach a man's hand if it be lowered in the water; but it is neat and thrifty in its habits: that is, it lays up stores in its nest, and, after eating up all that is eatable, it ejects the shells and sheaths of crabs and shell-fish, and the skeletons of little fishes. It seeks its prey by so changing its color as to render it like the color of the stones adjacent to it; it does so also when alarmed.*[3]

Aristotle dissected animals and described their internal organs. But he was equally interested in the behavior of living animals. It must have taken courage as well as patience to learn about the eating habits of the bear. He wrote that the bear:

. . . eats vegetables, and it will break up a hive to get at the honey; it eats crabs and ants also, and is in a general way carnivorous. It is so powerful that it will attack not only the deer but the wild boar, if it can take it unawares, and also the bull. After coming to close quarters with the bull it falls on its back in front of the animal, and, when the bull proceeds to butt, the bear seizes hold of the bull's horns with its front paws, fastens its teeth into its shoulder, and drags him down to the ground.[4]

He tells us that the lion "devours its food

Aristotle noted that the bear was a "powerful" animal, capable of attacking a deer, a wild boar, or even a bull.

greedily and fiercely."[5] Wolves never eat grass unless they are sick. Snakes can swallow eggs whole. Mice drink by lapping up the water. The beaver emerges from the water at nighttime and "goes nibbling at the bark of the aspens that fringe the riversides."[6] And finally, there was the hyena, which "is as large as a wolf, with a mane like a horse. . . . It will lie in wait for a man and chase him, and will inveigle [lure] a dog within its reach by making a noise that resembles the retching noise of a man vomiting."[7] He rounds off the description by saying that the hyena is very fond of rotten flesh and will burrow into a graveyard to satisfy its appetite.

Ecology is the study of the relationship between living things and their environment. It is looked on as a fairly recent branch of biology, but it actually dates back to the time of Aristotle. He was interested in how an animal's behavior was tied to searching for food and raising its young. He noticed how birds cope with changing seasons. Some stay in the same place, while others move to a warmer climate for the winter. He compared the wintering behavior of animals with that of people. Most seek shelter in their houses, but "men of great possessions spend their summer in cool places and their winter in sunny ones."[8]

He points out that in some cases birds "migrate from places near at hand, in others they may be said to come from the ends of the world, as in the case of the crane; for these birds migrate from the steppes of Scythia to the marshlands south of Egypt where the Nile has its source."[9] Aristotle must have learned this from well-informed travelers. He also observed that many fish migrate from deep waters to shallow waters with the change of the seasons.

In his *History of Animals*, Aristotle tried to cover everything that was known about animals. Some of the information was hard to come by because he was writing about animals from distant places. At other times he dealt with common creatures, such as honeybees. The Greeks were very familiar with bees, as honey was their only sweetener. It is no surprise then that Aristotle wrote at length about the life and habits of the honeybee. Much of what he writes

Aristotle must have interviewed many world travelers in compiling his notes on animals. He noted that the crane (above) migrated from the "steppes of Scythia to the marshlands south of Egypt."

is accurate, but not all. He claimed that, "In a high wind they carry a stone by way of ballast [balance] to steady them."[10] No one else has ever observed bees carrying stones. He also incorrectly believed that the hive was ruled by a king bee, and not a queen.

Despite some mistakes, Aristotle's knowledge of the animal kingdom is amazing. He did not merely describe animals. He wrote about their breeding habits, their structure, their range, and their relationship to other animals.

Alexander

IN 344 B.C., ARISTOTLE LEFT ASIA MINOR. King Philip of Macedonia had invited him to come to his court at Pella to teach Alexander, his thirteen-year-old son. The youth was intelligent and self-confident. One story goes that when he was only ten, he tamed a wild horse that none of the king's grooms could handle. King Philip had planned to buy the horse, but had changed his mind after watching his grooms try to mount it without success. Then Alexander asked if he could try. After quietly turning the horse to face the sun, the boy leapt onto its back and galloped off. He had noticed that when the grooms were

trying to mount, the horse was spooked by its own shadow. The more it reared, the longer and more frightening the shadow became. With its shadow behind it, however, the high-spirited animal was quite calm. Alexander named the horse Bucephalus. It would be his companion for the next twenty years.

The philosopher and the young prince formed close ties. They talked about politics and philosophy. Aristotle shared his interest in natural history with his pupil. He introduced him to the works of Homer, a Greek poet who lived in the eighth century B.C. Homer wrote two long poems—the *Odyssey* and the *Iliad*. The *Iliad* tells about Achilles and the Trojan War. At the start of the story, Achilles is angry with the Greek leader Agamemnon and refuses to continue fighting. When the tide of war turns in favor of the Trojans, Achilles' best friend Patrochus goes into battle disguised in the armor of Achilles. Patrochus slays many Trojan warriors, but is eventually killed by Hector of Troy. Achilles then rejoins the battle to avenge his friend's death. After some fierce fighting, he slays Hector.

Alexander loved the *Iliad*. The wild battle scenes probably appealed to him. He memorized most of the poem's 16,000 lines. Throughout his travels, he always slept with a copy under his pillow.[1]

When Alexander turned sixteen, Philip decided that there were other lessons his son needed to learn in order to be a successful king—he needed experience in the battlefield. So Alexander left Aristotle to join his father's army. The following year, mounted on Bucephalus, Alexander led a cavalry charge against the united armies of Thebes and Athens. King Philip led the foot soldiers. At one point, Philip's army pretended to retreat. The Athenian army followed. When it was crossing low ground, Philip turned and attacked again, trapping the Athenians between his foot soldiers and the cavalry.

In 336 B.C., when Alexander was twenty years old, his father was murdered and he became king. Some of his early actions show his respect for his former teacher. He gave orders that Aristotle's birthplace, Stagira, was to be rebuilt.

When he conquered Lesbos, he protected the island from looting by his soldiers because it was the home of Aristotle's friend, Theophrastus.

Now that he was in sole charge of the army, Alexander set off to conquer the known world. He had inherited his father's talent for organizing his troops. His huge following included more than soldiers. There were poets to entertain the troops and to write about the battles. Aristotle sent his nephew, Callisthenes,

This drawing shows Aristotle (right) teaching his most famous student, Alexander the Great.

along to record Alexander's adventures. There were also engineers, philosophers, geographers, and surveyors. And there were naturalists, who collected strange plants and animals, some of which were sent back to Aristotle. One historian describes Alexander's march across Asia as the first scientific expedition.[2]

One of the early stops was the city of Troy. As Alexander's ship drew close to the shore, he hurled his spear into the sand and leapt out after it. With a few close friends, including Callisthenes, he headed for the grave of the hero Achilles. There, he is said to have found several old pieces of armor—relics of the Trojan War. He carried them with him into battle to bring good luck.

In Gordium, a city in present-day Turkey, Alexander was invited to try to undo the Gordian knot, a tangled knot of bark tied to a chariot. The legend went that whoever undid the knot would become ruler of all Asia. Many people had already tried to untie the knot and failed. Alexander simply slashed through the tangle with one stroke of his sword, showing the keen mind and decisive action that would lead him to rule most of the known world.

Alexander founded cities that would play an important role in world history. One of the most important was Alexandria, a port city at the mouth of the River Nile in Egypt. It soon became a great center of commerce and learning. For the next thousand years, scientists and scholars visited its museum and library.

Back in 341 B.C., when Aristotle's tutoring job ended, he did not leave Pella right away. For the next five years, he lived either there or in Stagira. Little is known about his exact whereabouts, but it was during this time that he developed many of his original ideas. Freed from his teaching duties, he could spend his time in writing and in deep thought. He continued to make his observations on nature.

During these years Aristotle wrote *On Philosophy*, where he shows how his ideas differ from Plato's.[3] Then, in 335 B.C., the year after King Philip was murdered, he returned to Athens. He was now fifty years old. He was eager to share his wisdom.

The Lyceum

MANY CHANGES HAD TAKEN PLACE during Aristotle's twelve-year absence from Athens. The city was now under Macedonian rule. The Academy had changed, as well. Plato's nephew had died and the Academy had a new director. Aristotle, however, was not interested in returning to the Academy. Instead, he planned to set up his own school. He came well prepared. He had returned from his travels with a large number of books, maps, and teaching materials.

Because Aristotle was not a citizen, he could not own land in Athens. With Macedonian help, he rented a grove east of the city walls.[1] A temple to Apollo Lyceus, the wolf god, stood on the site, so his school became known as the Lyceum. Aristotle liked to walk up and down the covered walkway that led to the temple when he gave lectures. His students followed him closely, anxious to catch every word. This earned them the nickname Peripatetics, or walkabouts.[2] The Lyceum was often called the Peripatetic School.

The new school had two main goals—teaching and research. Although Aristotle is mostly remembered as a philosopher and scientist, he was also a good teacher. At the Lyceum, he taught both advanced and popular courses. Students at the Academy learned by Plato's method of discussion and argument, but Aristotle liked to lecture. He usually taught advanced students in the morning and the general public in the afternoon.[3] A number of his lecture notes have survived.

The Lyceum offered students more than just courses in philosophy and politics. Its wide choice of subjects made it more like the universities of today. Students from the Lyceum found jobs all over the world. In the first century B.C., the

Roman statesman Cicero wrote that "from the Peripatetic school, as from a factory producing specialists, there went forth orators, generals and statesmen, also mathematicians, poets, musicians and physicians."[4]

Aristotle wanted his students to learn about the natural world, so he set up a biological museum.[5] It contained specimens that Alexander sent him from his travels across Asia. He also gathered an outstanding collection of books. This library would become the model for the great library in Alexandria.

Aristotle surrounded himself with a team of able scientists and scholars. Among them was his friend Theophrastus from Lesbos. These scholars added to the vast amount of research done at the Lyceum. They followed Aristotle's scientific approach to solving problems. Aristotle said that the first step should always be to look at the history of earlier thought on the topic. Then one should look for reasons to doubt earlier solutions. After coming up with an answer of one's own, the next step was to look for evidence to support it. Although this method did not always lead Aristotle to the right conclusion, it marked a giant leap forward in the history of science.

Aristotle was the first person to use the science of logic. *Logic* comes from the Greek for "word." It is a form of reasoning. We use reasoning all the time without thinking of it as a science. If we arrive at the bus stop fifteen minutes late and no one is waiting, we conclude that we have missed the bus. If the line at the theater winds all the way around the block, we reason that it must be a popular movie. But Aristotle did not just jump to conclusions. He followed a precise line of thought in his reasoning.

One of Aristotle's contributions to the field of logic is known as *syllogism*. Syllogism deals with connections. If all A is B and all B is C, then it follows that all A is C. This is best described by giving a concrete example:

All owls are birds.

All birds have feathers.

So all owls have feathers.

We do not learn anything new from these

statements, but we have proved by this logic that owls have feathers.

Aristotle's development of logic was tied in with his interest in classifying things. He loved to make lists and sort things into categories. He listed the winners of the Olympic Games, for example. That was a simple task compared with bringing order to the world of nature. He recognized three main groups: animal, vegetable, or mineral. Out of these groups, his main interest was in the animal kingdom.

Meantime, Theophrastus took on the vegetables and minerals. He earned himself the name of "Father of Botany" by bringing order into the plant kingdom. In the *Account of Plants* he describes 550 species. He divided plants into trees, shrubs, undershrubs, and herbs. He also separated wild and cultivated varieties of plants. In his study of rocks, he distinguished between stones "of earthy origin" and metals.[6] He also made a detailed study of gems.

Aristotle thought that the earth was at the center of the universe. He based his conclusion on logic, but his reasoning was faulty. He argued

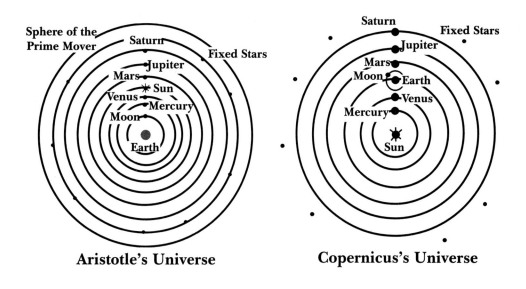

Aristotle's Universe

Copernicus's Universe

These diagrams show Aristotle's view of the universe compared with that of Copernicus.

that the earth could not be moving or we would feel the unsteadiness. We would also hear and feel the rushing winds. Although many people at that time thought the earth was flat, Aristotle believed that the earth was a sphere. Again, he used reasoning to reach this answer. He had noticed the way ships sink over the horizon. He had also observed the shadow of the earth during an eclipse of the moon.

Because Aristotle saw the heavens as unchanging, he had a problem with shooting stars and comets. They appeared to be far away, yet they were not predictable. Shooting stars (or meteors) only lasted for a second. Comets sometimes stayed in the sky for weeks, but then they, too, were gone. They were not a permanent part of the night sky like the stars and planets. He decided they must be part of the earth's upper air, along with clouds, wind, and rainbows. Although he was mistaken, it was a big step forward to understand that meteors and comets have a place in the natural world and are not the work of gods or demons. This science-based view of the world opened up a new way of thinking.

"A Desire for Knowledge"

WHILE ARISTOTLE WAS A TEACHER AT THE Lyceum, he still lived up to the name he had earned as a student at the Academy—the Mind. He brought new thinking to many branches of science. Back in the sixth century B.C., the famous mathematician Pythagoras and his followers thought that numbers were all-important. They gave numbers meanings outside of mathematics. For example, one stood for a point; two for a line; three for a surface; and four for a solid. Numbers took on other values as well. One was good and two was evil. A link to numbers still lingers in the meaning of words like *simplicity* and *duplicity*. Four was associated with justice. Today, a fair exchange is still often described as a "square deal."

Pythagoras tried to explain everything in terms of numbers, but Aristotle saw a distinction between mathematics and physics. Mathematics was an abstract science dealing with numbers and shapes. Physics was the science of how the world worked.

Aristotle brought his clear thinking to bear on many other problems that had interested earlier scholars. One was the problem of how things change. Aristotle separated change into four distinct ideas:

1) change of place (locomotion)
2) change of quality (alteration)
3) change of size (expansion or contraction)
4) change of substance

Aristotle described change of substance as "Coming-to-be and Passing-away."[1] He realized that in some cases when things were mixed together, they could be sorted out into their original form. Pebbles and shells, for example, can be mixed and then separated. In other cases,

In this medieval drawing, the ancient Greek philosopher and mathematician Pythagoras is shown (right) using an abacus. Unlike Pythagoras, Aristotle drew a distinction between the fields of mathematics and physics.

there is a change of substance. Tin and copper, once smelted into bronze, cannot be separated again. He was describing the difference between a physical change and a chemical change.

Aristotle's interest in change took him beyond the field of physics. He argued that when an object is altered, something causes the change. He gave the example of an object moving from "potentially hot" to "actually hot."[2] An outside force causes the change. Nature is full of examples of change: birth, growth, death, and decay. The life cycle of things on earth could be explained by the changing seasons. The changing seasons were caused by the motion of the heavenly spheres. But what caused the motion of the heavenly spheres? Aristotle suggested that an "Unmoved Mover" was the cause of motion that could not otherwise be explained. The Unmoved Mover was itself motionless and eternal. The Unmoved Mover was another name for God.

These abstract ideas are expressed in a collection of essays called the *Metaphysics*. In the first line of the *Metaphysics*, Aristotle says, "All men by nature have a desire for knowledge."[3] Our need to know is what separates us from other animals. It takes us closer to the Unmoved Mover. All animals relate to their surroundings through their senses. Some, such as the honeybee, cannot hear sounds, so they cannot learn, although they are intelligent.[4] Animals that have developed memory can learn. Experience and memory separate the human race from other animals. Humans live by art and reasoning.

Although the abstract ideas in the *Metaphysics* take one beyond physics, that is not the origin of the word. The name was given to the philosophical essays centuries later, simply because they came immediately after *Physics* in Aristotle's collected works. *Meta* is Greek for "after." The *Metaphysics* is the book that comes after the *Physics*.

Aristotle also wrote about ethics (rules of conduct). The most widely studied of his three books on ethics is the *Nicomachean Ethics*. It was probably written in honor of his father or to instruct his son—both were named Nicomachus.

Perhaps Aristotle was thinking about his son—or about himself in his younger days—when he wrote, "Youth will not receive a proper ethical training unless brought up under the right laws. To live a temperate and hardy life is not the choice of most people, especially the young. Therefore their upbringing and employments should be fixed by law."[5]

Aristotle believed that man's true goal in life is happiness. People who go after wealth or fame do so thinking that these things will make them happy. Happiness, on the other hand, is a final goal. People do not seek it as a step toward something else. He warns us, however, that we must not confuse happiness with pleasure: "Happiness is an activity of the soul according to goodness in a mature person."[6]

The ancient Greeks have given us some of the finest plays in literature. These include both comedies and tragedies. Among the most famous are the works of Sophocles and Euripides. In a world where the goal was happiness, how do tragedies fit in?

In *Poetics* Aristotle describes the structure of a

tragedy. It must consist of six parts—plot, character, diction, thought, spectacle, and song. The plot should focus on a single issue. Aristotle writes that the change in fortune "should come about as the result not of vice, but of some great error of frailty in a character."[7]

Aristotle pointed out that the difference between history and poetry is not that one is written in prose and the other in verse. Even if the works of the historian Heroditus were put into verse, it would still be history. The real difference is that one tells what has happened and the other tells what may happen. "Poetry, therefore, is more philosophical and a higher thing than history for poetry tends to express the universal, [and] history the particular."[8]

Aristotle decided that the value of tragedy is that emotions of pity and fear are purged or cleared away while one is watching a tragedy. This results in a sort of pleasure. Aristotle called this process "catharsis." This is the same experience that we get from watching a sad movie or reading a sad book.

Nowadays, we do not think of drama, politics,

and ethics as a part of science. A scientist's job is to inquire and find answers. Aristotle's goal was to understand. A person who had understanding was a scientist. Aristotle's definition of a scientist was very broad. It covered a person like himself who spent so much of his time thinking about thinking.

The End of the Road

WHILE ARISTOTLE WAS GUIDING HIS students into new ways of thinking at the Lyceum, his former pupil, Alexander, was changing the map of the world. By the time he was thirty years old, Alexander was Emperor of Greece, King of Persia, Pharaoh of Egypt, and Ruler of Asia. Some people even claimed he was a god. He marched his conquering army across Persia (what is now Iran), Afghanistan, and Pakistan, all the way to the Indus River.

Success on the battlefield did not come without cost to Alexander's character. As the victories piled up, his followers began to look on him with fear instead of respect. He had become so powerful that he could not stand having people disagree with him. One night, during a banquet, his friend Cleitus criticized him for adopting Persian dress. Alexander flew into a rage. He seized a spear and thrust it into Cleitus's heart—murdering the man who had once saved his life in battle.

Aristotle's nephew, Callisthenes, also lost his life because he spoke out against Alexander. Diogenes reports that Callisthenes was "confined to an iron cage and carried about until he became infested with vermin . . . and finally he was thrown to a lion and so met his end."[1]

Alexander waged his last battle in 326 B.C. against King Porus of India. Porus's troops were mounted on elephants. It took planning and cunning to defeat them. But it turned out to be a costly victory. Alexander's beloved horse Bucephalus died. The Greek biographer Plutarch wrote that Alexander was plunged into grief at losing his steed and companion.

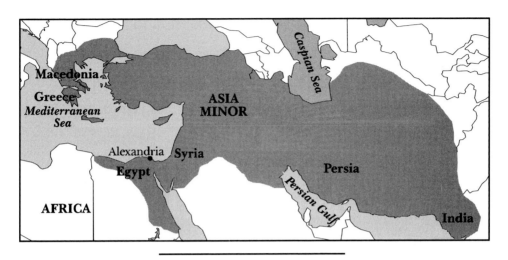

This map shows the boundaries of the empire of Alexander the Great (in dark gray) at its height.

Alexander founded the city of Bucephala in honor of the great horse's memory.[2]

King Porus was captured in the battle. When Alexander asked Porus how he wanted to be treated, Porus replied, "Treat me, Alexander, like a king."[3] Alexander was so impressed by this answer that he allowed Porus to continue to rule his kingdom. He even presented him with some new territory.

Alexander's soldiers were growing weary of fighting battles. They were tired of marching in the heat and the rain. They wanted to return to their families in Greece and Macedonia. Perhaps

Alexander, too, was tired of war. He turned his army back toward the west and began the long march home. However, he did not live to complete the journey. After surviving so many fierce battles, he died of a fever in Babylon in 323 B.C. The fever was probably malaria.

Alexander died without an heir. After his death, no one was strong enough to hold the mighty empire together. The empire eventually broke up into various countries, but not without a great deal of scheming and fighting. When news of Alexander's death reached Athens, angry feelings against the Macedonians flared up again. Patriotic Greeks turned on anyone who had had anything to do with the conquerors.

The citizens of Athens were aware of Alexander's contribution to the Lyceum. Aristotle's poem in memory of Hermias was looked upon as a sign of a lack of patriotism. Also, Aristotle was not an Athenian citizen. He became a target of their rage. History seemed to be about to repeat itself. Charges similar to those that were brought against Socrates were leveled at Aristotle. He did not wait for a trial. He fled with Herpyllis and his two children to Euboea, where he owned a house in Chalcis.

Theophrastus took over as director of the Lyceum. Aristotle gave him all of his books and research materials. It must have been a sad leave-taking. Not long after reaching Chalcis, Aristotle's health broke down. He died of a fever the following year in 322 B.C. He was sixty-two.

Aristotle wrote a will while he was in Chalcis. Aristotle's will reveals a great deal to us about his character. He comes across as a kindly man. He asked that his slaves be freed "when they arrived at the proper age."[4] He made plans for his daughter Pythias. He wrote: "when the girl shall be grown up she shall be given in marriage to Nicanor."[5] (Nicanor was the son of the uncle who had raised Aristotle after his parents died.) If something were to happen to Pythias—"which heaven forbid," Aristotle added—or if she should die without children, then Nicanor was to be her heir.[6]

Herpyllis and her son Nicomachus were well provided for. Aristotle writes of "the steady affection" which Herpyllis had borne towards him.[7] She was to be given to someone worthy if she should want to marry. In addition to receiving a talent of silver and three handmaidens, Herpyllis was given the choice of where to live. If she chose to remain at Chalcis, she was to be given the lodge by the gardens. If she wanted to return to Stagira, she was to have Aristotle's father's house. He went on to say, "Whichever of these two houses she chooses, the executors shall furnish with such furniture as they think proper and as Herpyllis herself may approve."[8]

An ancient bust of Aristotle.

Aristotle did not mention leaving his library to Theophrastus, nor did he mention the Lyceum. This is probably because he did not want to cause his friend or the school any trouble. At the time Aristotle wrote his will, he knew that feelings against him would still be running high.

Diogenes describes Aristotle as a man with a sense of humor. He gives examples of some of his "exceedingly happy sayings." When someone talked too much and then asked if they had bored Aristotle with their chatter, Aristotle would answer, "No indeed; for I was not listening to you." On the other hand, he was serious when it came to the value of teachers and education. He wrote that "Teachers who educated children deserved more honor than parents who merely gave them birth; for bare life is furnished by the one, the other ensures a good life."[9] He went on to say that the educated differed from the uneducated as much as the living from the dead. By this standard, Aristotle lived a very full life indeed.

His Writings Live On

LONG AGO, BOOKS WERE NOT LIKE THEY are today. Before the days of the printing press, they were written by hand. Making extra copies involved rewriting every word. The person making the copy sometimes made mistakes or sometimes even made changes on purpose.

In ancient Greece, the writing was done in columns on a long sheet of parchment, which is a kind of paper. The parchment was rolled sideways to form what is called a scroll. The reader unrolled the scroll as he read. Scrolls were not stored on shelves. Instead, they were usually kept in cubbyholes or in buckets. They were easily damaged, especially along the edges.

Because of this, only a small fraction of Aristotle's works has come down to us. None of the books that he wrote while he was at the Academy have survived. However, their contents are known because the books were not lost right away. Other ancient writers read them and quoted passages from them. All the books that survived, except for one, are lecture notes from Aristotle's teaching days in Assos, Pella, and the Lyceum. The exception is the *Athenian Constitution*. It was probably written while he was director of the Lyceum.[1]

There are two accounts of how the lecture notes survived. Both begin the same way, with Aristotle leaving his library to Theophrastus. When Theophrastus died, he willed the books to his nephew, Neleus. Neleus took them to his native city, Scepsis, in Asia Minor.

According to the first account, after Neleus died, his heirs sold some of the books to the famous library at Alexandria in Egypt. They did not want the rest of them to end up in a rival library that was being built closer to home in Pergamum, so they hid them in a cave.[2] The scrolls lay there for 200 years. A book collector named Apellico, who was passing through Scepsis, heard about the treasure in the cave. He tracked the scrolls down. He then took them to Athens, where he was putting together a private library.

The second account of the story is less exciting. Neleus's heirs did not hide the scrolls in a cave, but gave them or sold them to the

Aristotle's original writings were recorded on scrolls like the ones pictured above.

library in Pergamum. In this version the scrolls also ended up falling into the hands of Apellico. The book collector seems to have been a rogue. Earlier, he had been convicted of stealing city records in Athens. It seems likely that he invented the story of the cave to explain why he owned books that he had come by dishonestly.[3]

The text of the books is very complete. If the scrolls had lain in a cave for 200 years, many words and passages would have been hard to read for the person copying them. It appears that the scrolls had been cared for in a library. Also, scholars discussed the books during the time when they were supposed to be in the cave. This, too, is evidence that they were not hidden away, but were in a library where they could have been consulted.

In his biography of Aristotle, Diogenes records the names of all of Aristotle's books. He lists 156 titles.[4] Because several volumes appear under the same name, the total number of books actually adds up to over 360. Other scholars working with Aristotle probably wrote some of them. It is hard to compare the average length of a scroll with the average length of a present-day book, but Diogenes tells us that Aristotle wrote 445,270 lines.[5]

Most of Aristotle's books are known only as titles. The range of subjects that interested him is amazing. Here is a sample:

> Of Household Management, one book
> Of Wealth, one book
> Of the Soul, one book
> Of Friendship, one book
> Five books of Ethics
> Of Motion, one book
> Concerning Division, one book
> Definitions, thirteen books
> Politics, two books
> On Animals, nine books
> Concerning Astronomy, one book
> Eight books of Dissections
> Two books concerning Medicine
> Thirty-eight books of Physics
> Victors at Olympia, one book
> On Music, one book

Apellico's library in Athens was not the final resting place of the books. In 84 B.C., the Roman

Rembrandt painted Aristotle Contemplating a Bust of Homer *(above) in 1653. The piece demonstrates how the life and work of Aristotle continued to influence not only scientists, but artists as well, for many centuries after his death.*

general, Sulla, attacked the city. After a long siege, Athens fell. The victorious general ordered his soldiers to seize all of Apellico's books. They were then taken to Rome, where they were put under the charge of a librarian. For a few years no one bothered about them. Then a Greek philosopher named Tyrannio was brought to Rome as a captive. He became friendly with the librarian and was given the job of arranging Apellico's books. Tyrannio told Cicero, the famous statesman and writer, about Aristotle's scrolls. When Cicero read them, he realized that Aristotle was a great philosopher. Cicero helped spread Aristotle's fame.

Some time between the years 40 and 20 B.C., the scholar Andronicus of Rhodes took on the task of preparing a new edition of Aristotle's works. This is the version that has come down to us. With the publication of this edition, nearly 300 years after his death, Aristotle's place in history was secure. He would be honored as the greatest mind in science for the next 1,500 years.

Aristotle's Influence

ARISTOTLE WAS NOT THE FIRST SCIENTIST in ancient Greece, but many people look upon him as the greatest. Thales, who was a famous mathematician and astronomer, lived 300 years earlier. He traveled to Egypt, where he learned geometry. He thought that all things were formed from water and that the earth floated on water. Pythagoras, who died around 500 B.C., believed that understanding numbers was the key to all knowledge. About 100 years later, Democritus proposed the theory that every object was made up of lots of tiny atoms. Around the same time, Hippocrates was turning medicine into a branch of science.

Aristotle's logic was dominant from about A.D. 100 to 1870. His *Ethics* and *Poetics* remain influential to this day. Aristotle's lasting contribution in science was probably his work in zoology. It was not until the eighteenth century that anyone developed a better classification system. That was when Carl Linnaeus, a Swedish botanist, introduced the binomial system of nomenclature. This is a two-name system. Closely related plants or animals are given the same first name. It is the name of the genus. The second name describes the species. Plants and animals are given names in Latin, so that they are known by the same scientific name in all languages. For example, the scientific name for human beings is *Homo sapiens*. *Homo* is the Latin word for "man," and *sapiens* means "wise."

Charles Darwin, the great naturalist, was an enthusiastic fan of Aristotle. In 1882, a friend gave him a copy of a translation of Aristotle's *Parts of Animals*. In his thank-you letter, Darwin wrote: "I have rarely read anything which has

Swedish botanist Carl Linnaeus introduced the binomial system of nomenclature in the eighteenth century. Prior to that, Aristotle's system of animal classification had persisted for over two thousand years.

interested me more. . . . I had a high notion of Aristotle's merits, but I had not the most remote notion what a wonderful man he was. Linnaeus and Cuvier [a French naturalist] have been my two gods, though in very different ways, but they were mere schoolboys to old Aristotle."[1] Darwin went on to say that he never realized how much of our common knowledge we owe to Aristotle's work.

Aristotle was more successful as a biologist than as a physicist. Scientists often discover the answers to problems in physics by doing experiments. Aristotle did not try to prove his theories by doing experiments. This was not because he lacked equipment. For example, he could easily have tested the widely held idea that light objects fall more slowly than heavy objects do. People thought this because a feather floats gently to the ground while a heavy rock falls rapidly. If Aristotle had compared the fall of a flat piece of paper with the same size of paper crumpled into a tight ball, he would have found that under some conditions two objects that weigh the same can fall at different rates. This would surely have led to more questions and more experiments.[2] It would be a long time before anyone tackled the question of falling bodies. Galileo's experiment of dropping rocks from the Leaning Tower of Pisa was still 1,900 years in the future.

Aristotle is sometimes blamed for holding back the progress of science. This is because he was so respected that nobody dared to contradict him. Science might have moved forward faster if those who came after him had followed Aristotle's advice to his students. Remember, he told them to look at what earlier people had said on a given subject. Then they should look for reasons to doubt these ideas and come up with their own theory.

Progress in scientific thought was also delayed in the Middle Ages because it suited people to believe what Aristotle had taught. A good example is his theory that the earth is the center of the universe. This was the accepted belief in the Christian church. The theory was finally challenged by Copernicus, a Polish astronomer. He proposed that the earth circled around the sun. He delayed publishing his ideas until 1543 because he was afraid to disagree with the church. He died that same year. Almost 100 years later, Galileo was forced by a court of the Roman Catholic Church to take back his views on a sun-centered universe.

Aristotle wanted to know everything about the natural world. His interests ranged over a very broad field. He tried to discover rules that apply throughout nature. If he could not understand something, he did not fall back on explaining it as the work of gods, demons, or spirits. He looked for answers by making

Charles Darwin (above) was a great admirer of the scientific work of Aristotle.

observations, by collecting data, and by reasoning.

Within the last two centuries, science has taken us to heights undreamed of by Aristotle. Scientists have made huge strides in every field that Aristotle touched. But this is the age of the specialist. No one present-day scientist or philosopher can rival Aristotle in his ambition to know about everything.

Activities

Imitating Aristotle

Aristotle's search for knowledge was based on careful observation and good record keeping. He did not own a telescope or a microscope, nor did he have a calculator. So you do not need expensive equipment to follow in Aristotle's footsteps. All you need are an inquiring mind, keen eyes, and a record book.

When we want to learn about something we usually start by going to the library or searching the Web. We rely on other peoples' discoveries and knowledge. Aristotle would approve of this approach. His first step was to look at the history of earlier thought on any topic that interested him. Often, however, he was breaking new ground. He had to puzzle out an answer for himself. Finding something out for yourself can be rewarding, even when you are not the first person to come up with the answer.

The Night Sky

Long ago, people were much more aware of the stars than we are today. They could read the changing seasons in the night sky. Before there were artificial lights and smog, the sky was darker, so the stars appeared brighter. Today, most of us live in cities or towns, where streetlights dim the stars. So you might want to start your discoveries about the night sky by looking at the moon.

You do not need to be an astronomer to know that the moon changes shape. Sometimes it is a thin new crescent. Sometimes it is full. As the moon grows bigger, we say that it is *waxing*. As it grows smaller, it is *waning*.

Which way does the moon bulge when it is waxing? Does it bulge to the right like the letter "D" or to the left like a "C"? Check out your answer by observing the moon. You will need to follow it for several nights to tell if it is waxing or waning. The moon completes its cycle every month—or, more exactly, every twenty-nine-and-a-half days. How much later does it rise each night than the night before?

Once you have learned something about the movements of the moon, try stargazing. You are looking at the same stars that Aristotle observed. Many of the stars and constellations (groups of stars) have Greek names—names like Hercules and Orion. With the help of a star chart, see if you can identify some of the constellations. The Big Dipper and Orion are easy ones to start with.

The Busy Ant

Aristotle nominated the ant as one of the most industrious of all living creatures. He goes on to say that: "The way in which ants work is open to ordinary observation; how they all march one after the other when they are engaged in putting away and storing up their food; all this may be seen, for they carry on their work even during bright moonlit nights."[1]

Follow Aristotle's advice and observe ants as they forage for food and protect their young. Although most ants live in underground nests,

A nurse ant gathers up cocoons.

they are not hard to find. An ant's nest often looks like a mound of sandy soil with an opening on top. Others may be found under a flat stone. When you move the stone on a warm day, you are likely to see a lot of activity. Nurse ants dash about gathering up what appear to be eggs and quickly drag them into the underground tunnels. These "eggs" are actually cocoons that will soon become adults. Can you spot any soldier ants ready to defend the nest? You can recognize them by their big jaws.

When ants go out in search of food, they seem to be playing follow-the-leader. They lay down a scent trail from the nest to the food source. How do you think ants pick up the scent? What do they do if you rub away their invisible road? When two ants meet, they sometimes stop and pass on information. By watching carefully, you can find out how ants "talk" to one another (even if you do not know what they are saying!).

The Inhabitants of an Aquarium or Tide Pool

Aristotle was fascinated by marine animals. He was especially interested in the "bloodless" animals he found along the seashore near Assos and around the island of Lesbos. If you have the opportunity to visit an aquarium or a tide pool, make a list of all the marine animals you see. What features would you use to divide them into groups? Would you group sea anemones with the octopus because they both have tentacles? Does the hermit crab belong with the crabs or the sea snails? Aristotle puzzled over this. He wrote: "In its nature it resembles the crawfish kind . . . but by its habit of introducing itself into a shell and living there it resembles the testaceans [sea snails], and so appears to partake of the characters of both kinds."[2]

If you are not fortunate enough to live near the ocean or an aquarium, visit a pond. All you need is a dipping net or a sieve to discover some strange and interesting animals. Many of the squiggly things that live in fresh water are the young stages of insects.

Aristotle included spiders, centipedes, and scorpions in his insect group. Now insects are restricted to creatures with six legs, three body parts, and two antennae. But that only holds for adult insects. In some cases, the young stages are hard to recognize. They might easily be mistaken for worms.

Get Organized

Aristotle was a great list maker and organizer. He laid the foundation for zoology by "tidying up" the animal kingdom. He divided animals into groups. Some, like the hermit crab, were hard to place, but Aristotle was confident that everything in nature could be classified as animal, vegetable, or mineral.

Scientists who name and classify plants and animals are known as taxonomists. In everyday life, we classify objects without thinking of it as a branch of science. When we empty the dishwasher, we stack the plates on a shelf, hang the mugs on their hooks, put the bowls in the cupboard, and put the silverware in its drawer. There always seems to be few leftovers that do not fit the system, like spatulas and can openers.

In your own room, there is (probably) a place for everything. The next time you are told to tidy your room, remember Aristotle, the great organizer. Try taking a philosophical approach! Dirty clothes belong in the laundry hamper. Candy wrappers go in the wastebasket; empty soda cans are recycled. Eventually everything is in its place, except for a few leftovers. You may not know where they belong, but like Aristotle, you can be confident that they are animal, vegetable, or mineral.

Chronology

384 B.C.—Born in Stagira in northern Greece.

374 B.C.—His father, Nicomachus, dies. Proxenus of Atarneus becomes his guardian.

367 B.C.—Enters Plato's Academy in Athens.

347 B.C.—Death of Plato. Aristotle leaves Athens and travels to Assos to the court of Hermias in Asia Minor. Marries Pythias. Becomes interested in marine animals.

344 B.C.—Becomes tutor to Alexander.

341 B.C.—Alexander joins his father's army. Aristotle is relieved of his tutoring duties.

336 B.C.—Philip II is murdered.

335 B.C.—Alexander succeeds his father, Philip II, and sets out to conquer the known world. Aristotle returns to Athens and founds the Lyceum, a rival school to the Academy.

326 B.C.—Alexander reaches the gateway to India.

323 B.C.—Death of Alexander the Great and the breakup of his empire. Aristotle flees to Chalcis on the island of Euboea.

322 B.C.—Dies on Euboea, age sixty-two.

Chapter Notes

Chapter 1. Living in Interesting Times

1. George Sarton, *A History of Science*, vol. 1 (Cambridge, Mass.: Harvard University Press, 1952), p. 265.

2. Ibid.

3. Ibid.

4. Aristotle, "The Nicomachean Ethics," *Aristotle*, translated by Philip Wheelwright (Indianapolis: The Bobbs-Merrill Company, Inc., 1951), p. 227.

5. Ronald P. Legon, "Lyceum," *The World Book Multimedia Encyclopedia* (Chicago, Ill.: World Book, Inc., 1996).

6. Paul Strathern, *Aristotle in 90 Minutes* (Chicago, Ill.: Ivan R. Dee, Inc., 1996), p. 40.

Chapter 2. Aristotle's Childhood

1. Felix Grayeff, *Aristotle and His School* (New York: Harper and Row Publishers, Inc., 1974), p. 14.

2. Diogenes Laertius, *Lives of Eminent Philosophers*, vol. 2 (Cambridge, Mass.: Harvard University Press, 1966), p. 445.

3. Sarah B. Pomeroy, Stanley M. Burstein, Walter Donlan, and Jennifer Tolbert Roberts, *Ancient Greece: A Political, Social, and Cultural History* (New York: Oxford University Press, 1999), pp. 267–270.

4. Grayeff, pp. 15–16.

5. Laertius, p. 459.

6. Grayeff, p. 25.

Chapter 3. Athens, the City of Wonder

1. Sarah B. Pomeroy, Stanley M. Burstein, Walter Donlan, and Jennifer Tolbert Roberts, *Ancient Greece: A Political, Social, and Cultural History* (New York: Oxford University Press, 1999), pp. 275–276, 279.

2. Ibid., p. 279.

3. Ernest Barker, editor and translator, *The Politics of Aristotle* (London: Oxford University Press, 1961).

4. Thomas P. Kierman, editor, *Aristotle Dictionary* (New York: Philosophical Library, 1962), p. 512.

5. Ibid.

6. Pomeroy *et al.*, p. 216.

Chapter 4. The Academy

1. Diogenes Laertius, *Lives of Eminent Philosophers*, vol. 1 (Cambridge, Mass.: Harvard University Press, 1966), p. 155.

2. Ibid., p. 153.

3. George Sarton, *A History of Science*, vol. 1 (Cambridge, Mass.: Harvard University Press, 1952), p. 397.

4. Plato, *The Republic*, edited by G.R.F. Ferrari, translated by Tom Griffith (Cambridge, UK: Cambridge University Press, 2000), p. 314.

5. Sarton, p. 470.

6. Ibid., p. 471.

7. David C. Lindberg, *The Beginnings of Western Science: The European Scientific Tradition in Philosophical, Religious, and Institutional Context, 600 B.C. to A.D. 1450* (Chicago: University of Chicago Press, 1992), pp. 51–52.

8. Ibid., p. 57.

Chapter 5. A New Direction

1. Felix Grayeff, *Aristotle and His School* (New York: Harper and Row Publishers, 1974), p. 27.

2. Ibid., p. 28.

3. George Sarton, *A History of Science*, vol. 1 (Cambridge, Mass.: Harvard University Press, 1952), p. 471.

4. Thomas P. Kiernan, editor, *Aristotle Dictionary* (New York: Philosophical Library, 1962), p. 336.

5. Diogenes Laertius, *Lives of Eminent Philosophers*, vol. 2 (Cambridge, Mass.: Harvard University Press, 1966), p. 459.

6. Aristotle, *On Man in the Universe* (Roslyn, N.Y.: Walter J. Black, Inc., 1943), p. 49.

7. Aristotle, *The Works of Aristotle Vol. IV Historia Animalium*, translated by Darcy Wentworth Thompson (Oxford: Clarendon Press, 1910), V.32. 557b 1–2.

Chapter 6. The Father of Zoology

1. Aristotle, *The Works of Aristotle Vol. IV Historia Animalium*, translated by Darcy Wentworth Thompson (Oxford: Clarendon Press, 1910), II.1. 501a 24-25.

2. Ibid., VIII.2. 589b 5.

3. Ibid., IX.37. 622a 2–10.

4. Ibid., VIII.5. 594b 6–15.

5. Ibid., VIII.5. 594b 17.

6. Ibid., VIII.5. 594a 1.

7. Ibid., VIII.5. 594b 1–4.

8. Ibid., VIII.12. 596b 26–27.

9. Ibid., VIII.12. 597a 1–6.

10. Ibid., IX.40. 626b 24–25.

Chapter 7. Alexander

1. Robin Lane Fox, *Alexander the Great: A Biography* (London: Allen Lane, 1973), p. 59.

2. George Sarton, *A History of Science*, vol. 1 (Cambridge, Mass.: Harvard University Press, 1952), p. 490.

3. Thomas P. Kierman, editor, *Aristotle Dictionary* (New York: Philosophical Library, 1962), p. 8.

Chapter 8. The Lyceum

1. Felix Grayeff, *Aristotle and His School* (New York: Harper and Row Publishers, Inc., 1974), p. 38.

2. George Sarton, *A History of Science*, vol. 1 (Cambridge, Mass.: Harvard University Press, 1952), p. 492.

3. Ibid., pp. 492–493.

4. Grayeff, p. 39.

5. Ronald P. Legon, *The World Book Multimedia Encyclopedia* (Chicago, Ill.: World Book, Inc., 1996).

6. Sarton, p. 560.

Chapter 9. "A Desire for Knowledge"

1. Benjamin Farrington, *Aristotle* (New York: Frederick A. Praeger, Inc., Publishers, 1969), p. 74.

2. Aristotle, "The Metaphysics," *Aristotle*, translated by Philip Wheelwright (Indianapolis: The Bobbs-Merrill Company, Inc., 1951), p. 61.

3. Ibid., p. 67.

4. Ibid.

5. Farrington, p. 88.

6. Ibid., p. 91.

7. Aristotle, "The Tragic is Cathartic," *Classic Philosophical Questions*, ed. James A. Gould (Columbus, Ohio: Charles E. Merrill Publishing Co., 1985), p. 682.

8. Ibid., p. 680.

Chapter 10. The End of the Road

1. Diogenes Laertius, *Lives of Eminent Philosophers* (Cambridge, Mass.: Harvard University Press, 1952), p. 449.

2. N. G. L. Hammond, *The Genius of Alexander the Great* (Chapel Hill: University of North Carolina Press, 1997), p. 167.

3. Ibid.

4. Laertius, p. 459.

5. Ibid., p. 455.

6. Ibid.

7. Ibid., p. 457.

8. Ibid.

9. Ibid., pp. 461–463.

Chapter 11. His Writings Live On

1. George Sarton, *A History of Science*, vol. 1 (Cambridge, Mass.: Harvard University Press, 1952), p. 473.

2. Ibid., pp. 476–477.

3. Felix Grayeff, *Aristotle and His School* (New York: Harper and Row Publishers, Inc., 1974), p. 74.

4. Diogenes Laertius, *Lives of Eminent Philosophers*, vol. I. (Cambridge, Mass.: Harvard University Press, 1942), pp. 465–475.

5. Ibid., p. 475.

Chapter 12. Aristotle's Influence

1. George Sarton, *A History of Science*, vol. 1 (Cambridge, Mass.: Harvard University Press, 1952), p. 545.

2. John A. Moore, *Science as a Way of Knowing: The Foundations of Modern Biology* (Cambridge, Mass.: Harvard University Press, 1993), p. 40.

Activities

1. Aristotle, *The Works of Aristotle Vol. IV Historia Animalium*, translated by Darcy Wentworth Thompson (Oxford: Clarendon Press, 1910), IX.38. 622b 24–28.

2. Ibid., IV.4. 529b 22–25.

Glossary

Academy—The school in Athens that was founded by Plato.

acropolis—A high place in a Greek city.

agora—The marketplace in a Greek city.

binomial system of nomenclature—A two-word method of naming.

blooded—One of Aristotle's classes of animals. It corresponds to what we now call vertebrates (animals with backbones).

bloodless—The second of Aristotle's classes of animals. It corresponds to what we now call invertebrates (animals without backbones).

city-state—A political unit in ancient Greece.

democracy—Government by the people.

ecology—The study of the relationship between living things and their environment.

ethics—The study of moral principles.

logic—A method of reasoning.

Lyceum—The school in Athens founded by Aristotle.

Macedonia—A country to the north of Greece.

metaphysics—A branch of philosophy concerned with abstract ideas about truth and existence.

metic—A non-citizen.

Peripatetic School—Another name given to the Lyceum because the students walked about while they listened to lectures.

philosophy—The study of the principles and truths of being, knowledge, or conduct.

rhetoric—The ability to use language effectively.

species—A group of organisms that closely resemble one another and are able to interbreed.

syllogism—A form of argument that is supported by two statements.

theology—The study of God and religious faith.

tyrant king—A king with complete power.

Further Reading

Anderson, Margaret J., and Karen F. Stephenson. *Scientists of the Ancient World*. Berkeley Heights, N.J.: Enslow Publishers, Inc., 1999.

Barnes, Jonathan. *Aristotle*. New York: Oxford University Press, Inc., 2000.

Code, Alan D. *Aristotle*. Boulder, Col.: Westview Press, 2003.

Parker, Steve. *Aristotle and Scientific Thought*. Broomall, Pa.: Chelsea House Publishers, 1995.

Tames, Richard L. *Ancient Greek Children*. Chicago, Ill.: Heinemann Library, 2002.

Williams, Brian. *Aristotle*. Chicago, Ill.: Heinemann Library, 2002.

Woodfin, Rupert. *Introducing Aristotle*. New York: Totem Books, 2001.

Internet Addresses

Aristotle
http://www.ucmp.berkeley.edu/history/aristotle.html

Science and Human Values: Aristotle
http://www.rit.edu/~flwstv/aristotle1.html

Science in Ancient Greece
http://www.crystalinks.com/greekscience.html

Index